T0194811

PROVERBIAL TRUMP

PHINEHAS

WESTBOW
PRESS®
A DIVISION OF THOMAS NELSON
& ZONDERVAN

WestBow Press books may be ordered through booksellers or by contacting:

WestBow Press
A Division of Thomas Nelson & Zondervan
1663 Liberty Drive
Bloomington, IN 47403
www.westbowpress.com
844-714-3454

Scripture quotations taken from the (NASB®) New American Standard Bible®, Copyright © 1960, 1971, 1977, 1995, 2020 by The Lockman Foundation. Used by permission. All rights reserved. www.lockman.org

ISBN: 978-1-6642-6048-1 (sc)
ISBN: 978-1-6642-6049-8 (hc)
ISBN: 978-1-6642-6047-4 (e)

Library of Congress Control Number: 2022904574

Print information available on the last page.

WestBow Press rev. date: 03/28/2022

CONTENTS

Introduction. vii

Chapter 1 1
Viewing Donald Trump through the Word of
God Is the Best Thing for Our Nation

Chapter 2 5
Donald Trump Is Not All Bad

Chapter 3 8
George Washington's Farewell Address

Chapter 4 13
How Else Did We Become So Divided?

Chapter 5 17
Some Neuroscience behind Our Division

Chapter 6 23
Viewing Donald Trump through the Book of Proverbs

  PART 1: The Foundational Chapters of Proverbs (1-5)

  **PART 2: Viewing Donald Trump Through
      the Book of Proverbs (6-31)**

Afterword. 109
About the Author 115

INTRODUCTION

Decades ago, I became aware of Donald Trump as a brash, attention-seeking real estate developer. Then people from New Jersey made me aware of his several bankruptcies and pattern of not paying contractors for their work. A friend was one of those he cheated; in my friend's case, out of more than $50,000 in a Mexican real estate development. I don't watch much TV, and reality TV is nothing I spend much time on, so most of my awareness of Trump over the years came from the headlines on tabloids displayed near the checkout stand at grocery stores.

I did not support Trump in the 2016 presidential election because of my long-time awareness of his arrogantly immoral habit of using the courts to steal from others and his many lies driving the "birther" movement, denying and lying about President Barack Obama's qualifications to be president of the United States. When he was quoted saying that President Obama was the founder of the Islamic State (IS), I realized manipulating truth to meet his purpose was a consistent behavior—a prerequisite skill for a con man.

The main purpose of this book is to address our nation's increasing strife and division by viewing Donald J. Trump, the forty-fifth president of the United States, through the lens of scripture, particularly the book of Proverbs. Many Christians are supporters of Donald Trump, so let's shine the light of the word of God on his words and actions. This is not a book meant to condemn Donald Trump or those who are followers of Trump; it is to bring illumination of the scripture that leads to the light of the world, using that light as a lens to guide us to the blessings in the word of the Almighty God who loves us dearly. It's a quick read, and the supernatural aspect of God's word is amazing.

Over the last few decades, one of the first things I have done every morning is to study scripture. I start by reading a psalm, a chapter from the book of Proverbs, then one chapter from the books of the Bible, beginning from Genesis through Revelation, and then a chapter from one of the Gospels. When I reach the end of these, I start over at their beginning.

My favorite translation of the Bible is the Lockman Foundation's New American Standard (NASB 1995), the translation I have used for this book and generally considered to be a more scholarly translation into contemporary English. A 2020 edition of NASB has been published recently, but having begun writing this book in 2016, I decided to stick with the NASB 1995 and perhaps do a revision later. In this book, I have quoted scripture by book (such as Proverbs), chapter, and verse: Proverbs 6:16. Quotes from Jesus will be in **bold type**.

Whatever translation of the Bible a person reads, it is important not to isolate a verse from the context of the book, chapter, or surrounding verses. You can get a completely wrong interpretation from a verse by isolating it. You will notice that I didn't include many quotes referring to the behavior of kings; that's a different context. Many Christians don't study their Bible, but I can guarantee that the deeper you go into it, the deeper your faith will become, then the deeper your obedience, and the greater the joy of the Lord becomes a source of strength leading to a more tranquil temporal life and spiritual growth.

The motivation for this book began on November 9, 2016, when I awoke to the surprise that Donald Trump had been elected as the forty-fifth president of the United States. That morning in my daily study of scripture, I went on to read Psalm 12; when I reached the last two lines of verse 8, I was once again stunned by the supernatural aspect of scripture:

> The wicked strut about on every side when vileness is exalted among the sons of men.

I know the word of God guides me to the way, the truth, and the life, but I am always amazed when the supernatural timing of what I read aligns with specific events in my life; it grabs my attention and reveals things in amazing ways. This supernatural timing is a wonder to experience for anyone seeking the Lord through his word.

I then read Proverbs 9 and came to verses 7–8:

> He who corrects a scoffer gets dishonor for himself, and he who reproves a wicked man *gets* insults for himself. Do not reprove a scoffer, or he will hate you, reprove a wise man and he will love you.

Recalling Donald Trump's behavior during his campaign leading up to the 2016 election, I was surprised at how accurately these verses could be applied to him. After this, almost daily I was reading scripture that appeared to be pointing at Trump, and I became prayerfully compelled to share this with others, especially my family of the Christian church that were ignorant of what such scripture said and were blindly following the media outlets that supported Trump.

Another event that further encouraged me to continue writing this book occurred on the morning of October 7, 2019, when I read a Donald Trump tweet that stunned me. It was his reaction to an issue in Syria and began: "In my great and unmatched wisdom." Immediately I thought of Proverbs 26:12:

> Do you see a man wise in his own eyes?
> There is more hope for a fool than for him.

I must admit, he reminded me of the Wizard of Oz! I went on to read Isaiah 5:21:

> Woe to those who are wise in their own eyes
> and clever in their own sight!

I realize there will be many who will discount this book, but as Jesus said in Matthew 4:9, and also Luke 8:8, **"He who has ears to hear, let him hear."** And again in Matthew 4:23 He says, **"If anyone has ears to hear, let him hear."** (Note that I will be capitalizing pronouns referring to God the Father, Jesus, or the Holy Spirit.)

Please read through the parts that make might make you uncomfortable or appear to you as just "religious talk" so you can better grasp the supernatural power of God's word leading to good and away from evil. If the religious talk irritates you, just skip over it—there's plenty of interesting information ahead.

I have based most of my awareness of Donald Trump on reading his own tweets, watching his rallies and speeches, and listening to what he said—and not much on what others said *about* him. On the internet there is a multitude of quotes from Donald Trump, some presented as wise and inspirational, others in a less positive light. It's been said that the internet has a long tail, so they will be there for a long time, and there are many examples of Trump quotes that come to mind when studying the book of Proverbs. My comments were also influenced by books written by those who worked with Donald Trump and witnessed his behavior in the White House, such as John Bolton. I also studied quotes from the taped interviews that authors like Bob Woodward and Robert Costa had with him and transcripts of Trump's speeches, such as the one on January 6, 2021, in Washington, DC.

Some readers will disagree with my comments and even argue about their worth; that's understandable, as unlike Donald Trump, I don't claim to be a genius. However, please think about what each quotation from Proverbs brings to your mind. You can argue with me or what came to my mind, but can you really argue with the word of God?

1

VIEWING DONALD TRUMP THROUGH THE WORD OF GOD IS THE BEST THING FOR OUR NATION

> For the word of God is living and active and sharper than any two-edged sword, and piercing as far as the division of soul and spirit, of both joints and marrow, and able to judge the thoughts and intentions of the heart. (Hebrews 4:12)

What the US needs now more than anything is a revival that opens the eyes of our people to the incredible blessings God has for us when we turn to Him. George Washington knew that our country's birth was providential and its governance is dependent on God and His word when he said, "It is impossible to govern a nation without God and the Bible." He was not advocating a theocracy but pointing out that God's word is the best guide for a republic with democratic ideals.

Trump has claimed that the Bible is his favorite book, but when asked what some of his favorite verses of scripture are, he wouldn't quote one—he said that is "very personal." What? Sharing a favorite verse is a wonderful way of introducing the Gospel—think of John 3:16 as an example. However, several months later, he came up with favorite verses like "eye for an eye," and later he referred to "Two Corinthians," chapter 3, verse 17, which says, "Where the Spirit of Lord is, there is Liberty." Then there's his photo op holding up the Bible as a prop in front of St. John's Episcopal Church in Liberty Square. *What?*

The Old Testament has many examples of proud and wicked leaders who brought the nations of Israel and Judah to ruin, as in Ezekiel 14. We must learn from their mistakes. I urge those Trump supporters of the Christian or Jewish faith to study the Old Testament and/or the New Testament to see how wicked leaders and false prophets led to the destruction of great nations. Today's nation of Israel is a great example of God's loving-kindness, grace, and mercy for those who do return to Him.

As scripture calls us to pray for those in authority, I prayed for Donald Trump as the president of the United States. It is not my responsibility nor place to judge Him. I too am a sinner. In this book, I simply want to share what scripture says, primarily the book of Proverbs, and what sense it makes when applied to Trump. If someone can still support Trump's greed for power and wealth after knowing how many lines of scripture, particularly the book of Proverbs, show that he and those like him are not what God is pleased with, they do so not only at their own peril but at the peril of the United States of America too.

Sometimes people are uncomfortable when the Bible tells us to fear the Lord; many people wonder, "If the Lord loves me, why should I fear Him?" The book of Proverbs helps us understand this a little better. The English word *fear* translates a term that also means "revere" or "honor." There is nothing more powerful than the Creator of the universe! God's nature is loving-kindness beyond our imagination, and we feel it when we observe its beauty, but it is also powerful and wildly dangerous beyond our imaginations; the violence from colliding galaxies makes any natural disasters on earth pale in comparison. However, that is just physical destruction. What about our spirits?

In Luke 12:4–5, Jesus says,

> **"I say to you, My friends, do not be afraid of those who kill the body and after that have no more that they can do. But I will warn you whom to fear: fear the One who, after He has killed, has authority to cast into hell; yes, I tell you, fear Him!"**

But never forget He loves you so much that He gave His Son, Jesus, to redeem you from sin, and your acceptance of that gift is what saves you from eternal separation from

God, which is hell. It is His will that you join Him in heaven, but He doesn't force His will on you; you can ask that His will be done or follow your own will. The love of God is a choice, not an uncontrollable reflex. He chooses to love us, but not all of us choose to love Him. Also, be sure to note that there are Bible verses that explain what God hates. Proverbs 13:8 says,

> The fear of the LORD is to hate evil; Pride and arrogance and the evil way and the perverted mouth, I hate.

It's hard not to think about Trump's pride and arrogance when you consider that verse.

2

DONALD TRUMP IS NOT ALL BAD

> The LORD has made everything for its own
> purpose, even the wicked for the day of evil.
> (Proverbs 16:4)

Do not interpret this writing as an attempt to present Donald Trump as a person who represents nothing good. God might not approve of what he does, but He still loves him. Many people have been praying for him. As I said, I too am a sinner. I don't believe I can judge Trump, but God's word can. Also, I would be remiss if I didn't say I think the Trump administration did achieve some beneficial outcomes for the United States. For example, the audit of the Defense Department in 2018 has improved the accountability of the Pentagon's management of its budget. Regulating robocalls was another move in the right direction. There was a closer look at the possible negative impacts of Chinese technology and efforts to prevent its use against the US. Although Trump lied about the rising numbers of cases and deaths related to COVID-19, saying it was "totally under control" and would disappear with warmer weather, he said he did so because he didn't want people to panic. Also, Trump eventually used the Defense Production Act to increase the production of ventilators for people suffering from COVID. Best of all, he did at least ask the nation to pray about it.

Building a border wall and having Mexico pay for it was a failing solution, but Trump did keep attention on our immigration problems. The issue of abortion is another area that Trump sought to address. I was also impressed by an old *Reader's Digest* story about him paying off the mortgage of a good Samaritan who gave his limo roadside assistance during a snowstorm.

Trump's moving of the US Embassy to Jerusalem was also something I appreciate; if you have ever been there, you can sense that it is God's city. Sitting on the Mount of Olives and praying as I watched dawn come over Jerusalem gave me a feeling of awe I won't forget. It is no coincidence that three of the world's major religions, all deriving from Abraham, vie for the city.

Trump's move to appoint conservative Supreme Court justices brought a more conservative court; thank God, they saw through Trump's fraudulent 2020 presidential election lies that he spread in his attempt to overturn our democratic republic's principles for a peaceful transfer of power. So far, the Supreme Court of the United States appears to be continuing a swing of the pendulum away from the fairly liberal court of the mid to late twentieth century. However, its "shadow docket" practice is cause for concern; we will need to keep an eye on that.

On a more humorous note, today Trump let me know that if I send him $45 before the end of the day, I can join other patriots by getting a personalized Official Trump Card! Also, if I send him more money, I can get a football signed by him. As if these cons weren't obvious enough, I received another con from Team Trump around Christmas that said: "Just contribute $75 NOW and we'll send you one of our ICONIC Trump Save America Christmas Ornaments for FREE." I pay $75 and get it for FREE? I guess I'm not naïve enough to bite on that one. Anyone who doesn't see this as a con artist's ploy needs to open their eyes to God's word.

3

GEORGE WASHINGTON'S FAREWELL ADDRESS

I am not a Republican, and I am not a Democrat. I am an American. I am an American who understands what George Washington, one of our nation's greatest founding fathers, warned us of in his in his Farewell Address: divisiveness caused by political parties. Our nation's widespread ignorance of his warning is a major cause of the decline of America's power. George Washington did not consider himself an educated man, compared to several other founders, but he did try to make up for that in his writing; although the ideas were his, Alexander Hamilton and James Madison helped him write his farewell address. I believe it to be one of the most important writings for uniting and protecting our nation, yet very few Americans are aware that Washington warned us not to do exactly what we have been doing!

Here is a portion of his address that particularly describes what causes divisiveness in United States of America today: political parties.

> I have already intimated to you the danger of parties in the State, with particular reference to the founding of them on geographical discriminations. Let me now take a more comprehensive view, and warn you in the most solemn manner against the baneful effects of the spirit of party generally.

> This spirit, unfortunately, is inseparable from our nature, having its root in the strongest passions of the human mind. It exists under different shapes in all governments, more or less stifled, controlled, or repressed; but, in those of the popular form, it is seen in its greatest rankness, and is truly their worst enemy.

> The alternate domination of one faction over another sharpened by the spirit of revenge, natural to party dissension, which in different ages and countries has perpetuated the most horrid enormities, is itself a frightful despotism. But this leads at length to a more formal and permanent

despotism. The disorders and miseries which result gradually incline the minds of men to seek security and repose in the absolute power of an individual; and sooner or later the chief of some prevailing faction, more able or more fortunate than his competitors, turns this disposition to the purposes of his own elevation, on the ruins of public liberty.

Without looking forward to an extremity of this kind (which nevertheless ought not to be entirely out of sight), the common and continual mischiefs of the spirit of party are sufficient to make it the interest and duty of a wise people to discourage and restrain it.

It serves always to distract the public councils and enfeeble the public administration. It agitates the community with ill-founded jealousies and occasionally riot and insurrection. It opens the door to foreign influence and corruption, which finds a facilitated access to the government itself through channels of party passions. Thus, the policy and the will of one country are subjected to the will of another.

There is an opinion that parties in free countries are useful checks upon the administration of the government and serve to keep alive the spirit of liberty. This within certain limits is probably true; and in governments of a monarchial cast, patriotism may look with indulgence, if not favor, upon the spirit of party. But in those of the popular character, in governments of purely elective, it is a spirit not to be encouraged. From their natural tendency, it is certain that there will always be enough of that spirit for every salutary purpose. And there is constant danger of excess, the effort ought to be by force of public opinion, to mitigate and assuage it. A fire not to be quenched, it demands a uniform vigilance to prevent its bursting into flame, lest instead of warming, it should consume.

It helps to read Washington's warning again. It should be required reading in our nation's schools. Consider today's average person; will they even understand whom or what danger that Washington, in his wisdom, is describing? I have provided only a portion of the Farewell Address, but if we want to maintain the unity that makes our country exceptional, we must all be aware of the warning he presents. It is a very accurate description of how we need to come together and reject anyone who attempts to pit one part of our nation against another, as Trump so blatantly has done or continues to do in his tweets, speeches, and rallies and through conservative media. I don't consider myself a conservative or a liberal American. As it says in Proverbs 4: 25–27:

> Let your eyes look directly ahead and let your gaze be fixed straight in front of you. Watch the path of your feet and all your ways will be established. Do not turn to the right nor to the left; turn your foot from evil.

It's interesting that this not turning to the right or left is mentioned several times in the Bible. Much of the political discourse and information in the US has become slanted; the more our sources of information are at the extreme ends of the spectrum of conservative to liberal, the less credible they are. There are many on both ends of the media spectrum who know its power to persuade, especially through words that stir emotion.

4

HOW ELSE DID WE BECOME SO DIVIDED?

There are many roots of our nation's divisiveness. Democratic republics are difficult to hold together, but even more so now that technology-driven information has become a tool to divide and conquer by using wedge issues to drive people apart. Wedge issues are things like abortion, taxes, and the rights of those not like us, whether in regard to race, sexuality, religion, income level, political party, or identity on the conservative-liberal spectrum. Decades ago, politicians become very shrewd in using wedge issues to divide us, but now, with technology and social media, information sources have become superspreaders for wedge issues. Some media that claim to be news actually don't report news; they are digital tabloids, and their purpose is to use bits of news as wedge issues to sway opinion for one political party or another. They are exactly what George Washington warned against.

Wedge issues became a way for politicians to adopt one side and attack those on the other side as being bad people on the principle of "they don't agree with us, so they must want to ruin our country." Wedge issues are used especially to inflame opinion in those who identify as Christians; for example, dividing voters along religious lines has been a very successful way of influencing the agenda of school districts. Deceitful politicians claiming to be Christians used wedge issues to get religious organizations to endorse them, and too many in church leadership took the bait hook, line, and sinker, encouraging their followers to vote according to a list of candidates recommended by their religious organizations. I am reminded of Jesus quoting the prophet Isaiah in Mathew 12:8–9:

> **"This people honors Me with their lips, but their heart is far away from me. But in vain do they worship me, teaching as doctrines the precepts of men."**

In the last decade, just as George Washington warned us, foreign countries have been using wedge issues to divide us; they know that when the US is united, it is the most powerful nation in the history of the world. Russia has been very busy dividing our nation using wedge issues and (un)social media. And wedge issues lead to wedge labels; I'm amazed at how quickly Trump supporters call me a Democrat because I can't support Donald Trump. *Wrong.*

Trump uses the same technique of wedge issues and labels. On February 3, 2020, at the National Day of Prayer Breakfast in Washington, DC, at what had been for forty-seven years a time for bipartisan prayer in reverence for God's blessings on our nation and requests for a greater unity to trust in Him, Trump instead took the opportunity to attack his political opponents, belittling their faith and lack of support for him. I was sadly amazed at the Christian leadership who ignored this shift from uniting in humble prayer to spreading strife in our nation.

Many who claim to be followers of Jesus have become followers of Trump. However, they spend much more time, effort, and money supporting Trump than they spend following Jesus! If you support Donald Trump, add up the amount of time you spend listening to Trump or pro-Trump politicians or media, and ask yourself: is it more or less than the time you spend with God's word? After reading this book, you will see, I hope, that the confidence of Trump's supporters is built on the sand foundation of their own ignorance of what God's word says in Proverbs.

However, we must stop being religious in a way that allows our relationship with God the Father, Jesus, and the Holy Spirit to be used by politicians as a political weapon or wedge issues to get votes. Instead, we must be spiritual in a way that allows others to see our relationship with Jesus and the fruits of the Holy Spirit in our words and actions. This influence is much more powerful than scoffing at those who don't think as we do. Too many people criticize Trump's followers for their invincible ignorance when they should be sharing God's word that brings light to the way, the truth, and the life: Jesus!

What brings us together in the first place is an understanding of who our common enemy is, or a common purpose. The monarchy we wanted to leave behind when this country was created reacted in ways that motivated us even more strongly to leave it. Today, the party system is using media to paint those Americans who disagree with us as our enemy that should be destroyed before they take away our rights. We must focus on being united rather than divided!

5

SOME NEUROSCIENCE
BEHIND OUR DIVISION

> An amygdala hijack is an emotional response
> that is immediate, overwhelming, and out of
> measure with the actual stimulus because
> it has triggered a much more significant
> emotional threat. (Wikipedia)

Technology's influence on the science of communication
has created a symbiotic and synergistic effect to greatly
increase the impact of media on everyone, particularly
those ignorant of this insidious force in driving
widespread opinion. The stronger the ignorance, the
stronger the opinion. Over the last few decades, as
technology and media have influenced communication
throughout the world, it appears that more and more
people are unaware of what tech and media have done
to their brains.

Increasingly powerful brain imaging shows us the amygdala, a small but powerful part deep in our brain, close to the brain stem, that is the source of our emotions. "Hijacking" the amygdala can initiate the flight or fight response, which keep us from using the frontal lobes—the thinking, rational parts of our brain. Both conservative and liberal media use this tactic. The overwhelming increase of information, combined with media awareness of how to harness the amygdala to keep the brain disgusted, fearful, and/or angry, prevents our brains from thinking clearly or spiritually.

Sound bites that can be repeatedly shouted at others strengthens the neural connections of those who believe what is said, but they contribute nothing to the dialogue with those who don't already believe. Notice the emotional shouting of the pundits transmitting the disdain, disgust, fear, or rage they want the listener to have. Back in the 1980s, Rush Limbaugh became extremely good at this tactic, leading to many "shock jocks" stirring up the opinions of their listeners. Beginning in the mid-1990s, Fox News became exceptionally effective in using this tactic and became the desired information source for those who identify as conservatives. The media have evolved from the red herrings of yellow journalism, to radio talk shows, to websites and apps or podcasts that stir large groups of people into action through emotion. Pundits are amygdala cowboys trying to create emotionally political stampedes.

I am amazed at the websites people are believing—or rather, emoting from. There is neuroscientific research that leads us to a concept referred to as "mirror neurons," meaning that we mirror what is happening in the brains of those we observe. An initial awareness of this phenomenon in neuroscience occurred when a neuroscientist walked into a lab with monkeys that had their brains wired to show patterns of neural activity. It was a warm day, and the scientist was eating an ice cream cone as he entered and walked through the lab. He was amazed at the sudden burst of activity shown on the monitors, signaling that the monkeys' brains were firing in the neural areas associated with eating an ice-cream cone, mirroring his own neurons!

This is why those on the ends of the ultra-liberal or ultra-conservative spectrum become so emotional when they come together; whether it is a Trump rally, the QAnon movement, or a Portland protest, or even a stadium full of sports fans, the mirror neurons are powerful in stimulating the amygdalae. This can happen electronically as well, but not with as much power as face to face. Proverbs 27:19 says, "As in water face *reflects* face so the heart of man *reflects* man" (emphasis mine). Trump rallies show the power and effects of neuron mirroring, and in particular the attack on our Capitol on January 6, 2021—it is the source of the "mob mentality" that many of the January 6 insurrectionists or rioters have claimed is patriotism motivating them. However, George Washington warned us to "guard against the intended impostures of patriotism."

Mirror neurons are not always a negative thing. A great, enthusiastic teacher can make learning enjoyable by firing up the amygdala of the learner through mirror neurons. Houses of worship are a prime source of mirror neuron activity, spreading the joy of the Lord. Emotional memories are easier to retain.

Information Sources

So how do we get our news? I try to get the facts online by scanning curations of headlines from news outlets such as Reuters or the Associated Press, or Google News. The curations contain both conservative and liberal media. Reading can supply information better than listening to a speaker because you can quickly reread something to better comprehend it, while the speaker just keeps on giving you something else to think about—or more to the point, to *feel*. However, even print can be loaded with adjectives to get your amygdala engaged.

There is a game I play with my wife sometimes. I read three headlines and ask her to identify which media organization wrote them. She has become very good at discerning the source of headlines from Fox News or other right-leaning, tabloid-style media—they usually contain more negatively emotive adjectives. It is a major reason I do not *watch* news; the facts can be assessed with a quick read, and it is easier to identify facts when they are not colored by the adjective-laden spin that guides amygdala activity.

Technology's impact on media has grown over the last few decades, and it has increased the speed and amount of misinformation and propaganda spreading throughout our nation. Much of this comes from the influence of foreign governments, as predicted by George Washington, and has been identified by our nation's intelligence agencies. Trump apparently has tried to create his own media source to control the tools of control, and although he is still able to fleece his supporters for money, it has not been successful on a large scale. His frequent claims that any news putting him in a bad light was "fake news" brought the power of his mendacity to a much higher level.

More and more people are asking the question Pontius Pilate posed to Jesus before He was crucified, "What is truth?" (John 18:38), when truth was standing right in front of him. The strife and division growing in the US can be healed by our Lord, as shown by the amazing achievements of our nation when we do seek Him. It's geometric growth: as we draw nearer to the Lord, we draw nearer to one another, and cohesiveness prevents divisiveness.

During the several years it took to write this book, I was increasingly amazed at how Trump's actions over the course of his time in office became more and more wicked as he systemically undermined the press, Congress, the courts, the Justice Department, intelligence agencies, and any institutions limiting his power. Along the way, I read more and more scripture that describes the situation that our own nation is now in. The many verses in the Bible that appear to point to God's disapproval of leaders like Trump could make a whole other book.

I have not provided footnotes for the behaviors and quotes of Donald Trump in commenting on the many passages in Proverbs that connect with them. They are well known, and readers can readily verify them on the internet. I believe that doing so will help those reading this book to become more aware of the variety of information sources and to discern between those reporting news and those spinning facts to elicit emotional reactions.

6

VIEWING DONALD TRUMP THROUGH THE BOOK OF PROVERBS

Part 1: The Foundational Chapters of Proverbs (1-5)

The first few chapters of the book of Proverbs set the stage for understanding how valuable they are for guiding our nation and how many of Trump's strongest behavioral traits can be viewed in light of Proverbs. Also addressed is the consequence of ignoring the word of the Lord. I have proceeded through the book of Proverbs by chapter, calling readers' attention to verses that seem most illuminating.

Proverbs 1

Let's begin with the first chapter of Proverbs, verses 2–5.

> To know wisdom and instruction,
> To discern the sayings of understanding,
> To receive instruction in wise behavior,
> Righteousness, justice and equity;
> To give prudence to the naïve,
> To the youth knowledge and discretion,
> A wise man will hear and increase in learning,
> And a man of understanding will acquire
> wise counsel.

It is well known, especially by those who have been in Trump's Cabinet, that he preferred to follow his instincts than to listen to counsel.

> The fear of the LORD is the beginning of knowledge; fools despise wisdom and instruction. (Proverbs 1:7)

As noted in chapter 1, "the fear of the Lord" can be interpreted as "reverence." This reverence opens our eyes to knowledge in God's word that can lead to wisdom. According to his own words, Trump trusts his own instincts rather than the instruction or counsel of his advisors. As you read on, Proverbs makes it clear that Trump, despite his claim to being a genius, is a fool.

> How long, you naive ones, will you love simplistic thinking?

And *how long will* scoffers delight themselves
in scoffing and fools hate knowledge? (1:22)

It is anyone's guess how long or why Trump supporters
are drawn to his simplistic views and scoffing. Defined
as "contemptuous ridicule or mockery of someone or
something," *scoffing* is a word that is not often used today,
but it certainly is a trait Trump exhibits often. I see it in
his followers as well. His supporters do have a choice to
stop such behavior. What happens if they continue their
ignorance of the Lord's word and continue to follow
Trump's example?

Turn to my reproof,
Behold, I will pour out my spirit on you;
I will make my words known to you. (1:23)

Praise God for His merciful amazing grace! The next
four verses describe the consequences of ignoring His
word.

Because I called and you refused, I stretched
out my hand and no one paid attention;
And you neglected all my counsel and did
not want my reproof;
I will also laugh at your calamity; I will
mock when your dread comes,
When your dread comes like a storm and
your calamity comes like a whirlwind,

when distress and anguish come upon you.
(1:24–27)

Does this describe just our storms and fires, or climate change?

Then they will call on me, but I will not
answer; they will seek me diligently but they
will not find me,
Because they hated knowledge and did not
choose the fear of the LORD.
They would not accept my counsel, they
spurned all my reproof.
So, they shall eat of the fruit of their own
way and be satiated with their own devices.
(1:28–31)

Remember, Jesus taught us to pray **"Your will be done."**
However, if we insist, he will let our will be done—along
with the consequences.

For the waywardness of the naïve will kill
them, and the complacency of fools will
destroy them. (1:32)

How many of our fellow Americas were naïve enough
to believe Trump's dismissive scoffing at the COVID-19
pandemic, and paid with their lives?

But he who listens to me shall live securely
and will be at ease from the dread of evil.
(1:33)

A revival of following God's word is something our
nation needs desperately. Following leaders like Trump
has brought us to this state of division that we are in. It
is not too late to return to the Lord! The Bible has many
examples where cities or nations are saved by repenting
from following idols, and God's mercy was given to
them.

Proverbs 2

The second chapter of Proverbs continues to show us
the benefits and wisdom of fearing the Lord rather than
following leaders like Trump who model behaviors never
recommended by the Lord.

Make your ear attentive to wisdom, incline
your heart to understanding;
For if you cry for discernment, lift your
voice for understanding;
If you seek her as silver and search for her as
for hidden treasures;
Then you will discern the fear of the
LORD and discover the knowledge of God.
(Proverbs 2:2–5)

Discerning the fear of the Lord does not lead to being afraid of Him; it is the reverence for the majesty and glory of the Lord that brings joy from knowing we are loved beyond our imagination by the Almighty, and this "Joy of the Lord is their strength" (Nehemiah 8:10).

> For the LORD gives wisdom; from His mouth *come* knowledge and understanding. (Proverbs 2:6)

It is in His word to be found by those who seek it.

> He stores up sound wisdom for the upright;
> *He is* a shield to those who walk in integrity,
> Guarding the paths of justice, and He watches over the way of His godly ones. (2:7–8)

Thank God he thwarted Trump's attempted manipulation of our courts.

> Then you will discern righteousness, justice, integrity, and every good path.
> For wisdom will enter your heart, and knowledge will be delightful to your soul;
> Discretion will watch over you, understanding will guard you,
> To rescue you from the way of evil, from a person who speaks perverse things. (2:9–12)

Trump's quote about grabbing women by their genitals is certainly perverse. How can his supporters ignore this?

> From those who leave the paths of uprightness
> to walk in the ways of darkness;
> Who delight in doing evil and rejoice in the
> perversity of evil;
> Whose paths are crooked, and who are
> devious in their ways;
> To deliver you from the strange woman,
> from the adulteress who flatters with her
> words. (2:13–16)

Trump certainly had quite a lot of media and trouble with this one.

Proverbs 3

The third chapter of Proverbs begins with the basics of seeking God; for those who memorize scripture, these verses could be considered as the place to start a walk with the Lord.

> Do not let kindness and truth leave you;
> bind them around your neck, write them
> on the tablet of your heart. (Proverbs 3:3)

Kindness and truth are not Trump's strong traits.

> So you will find favor and good repute
> In the sight of God and man.
> Trust in the Lord with all your heart and
> do not lean on your own understanding.
> (3:4–5)

Or instincts.

> In all your ways acknowledge Him, and He
> will make your paths straight. (3:6)

Not to the left or the right.

> Do not be wise in your own eyes; fear the
> Lord and turn away from evil. (3:7)

On October 7, 2019, when I read "In my great and unmatched wisdom" in Trump's tweet, I thought of this proverb and wondered how Christians supporting him would react. They didn't. Many self-professed Christians following Trump have made him their idol, paying more attention to his words than the Lord's word—a pattern of behavior that always leads a nation to strife, suffering, and destruction.

> For the devious are an abomination to the
> Lord; but He is intimate with the upright.
> (3:32)

Trump's history of devious schemes and lies truly make him an abomination. An "abomination" is something regarded with disgust or hatred; in this verse, that is how the Lord views the devious. "He is intimate" can be literally as "His private counsel," which is a great description for the word of God.

> Though He scoffs at the scoffers, yet He gives grace to the afflicted. (3:34)

It amazes me how those individuals and media who become supporters of Trump exhibit his scoffing behavior. However, it is clear that many who oppose Trump scoff right back at his supporters. Don't forget: the Lord scoffs at those who exhibit scoffing behavior.

> The wise will inherit honor, but fools display dishonor. (3:35)

The word "display" could also be interpreted as "raise high." This verse brings to mind the way Trump would give praise and recognition to Putin, or award the Presidential Medal of Freedom to someone like Rush Limbaugh, who spent much energy in mean-spirited scoffing and publicly dishonoring others who didn't agree with his political views. Limbaugh was a great example of just what George Washington warned against.

Proverbs 4

This chapter is mostly a father's instructions.

The following passage from chapter 4 of Proverbs reminds me of the deceitful tweets or retweets that would come from Trump at all hours of the night.

> Do not enter the path of the wicked and do not proceed in the way of evil people.
> Avoid it, do not pass by it; turn away from it and pass on.
> For they cannot sleep unless they do evil; and they are robbed of sleep unless they make *someone* stumble.
> For they eat the bread of wickedness, and drink the wine of violence. (Proverbs 4:14–17)

Trump's photo op at Lafayette Square?

> But the path of the righteous is like the light of dawn that shines brighter and brighter until the full day. (4:18)

That path of righteousness can be found in the Bible; the more you study it, the brighter it shines.

> The way of the wicked is like darkness; they do not know over what they stumble. (4:19)

These are dark times, and the masses are confused over what is good and what is evil, making it easier for deceitful con men to mislead many.

> Rid yourself of a deceitful mouth and keep devious speech far from you. (4:24)

Many Trump supporters simply repeat what they have heard from deceitful media pundits.

> Do not turn to the right or to the left; turn your foot from evil. (4:27)

Here again, the Bible tells us to make our path straight.

Proverbs 5

This chapter addresses the pitfalls of immorality.

No other president of the United States has been impeached twice. It remains to be seen how Trump's tax returns might become iniquities.

> His own iniquities will capture the wicked, and he will be held with the cords of his sin. He will die for lack of instruction, and in the greatness of his folly he will go astray. (Proverbs 5:22–23)

Trump doesn't like to read and often claimed he preferred his own instincts to the advice of his cabinet members.

Part 2: Viewing Donald Trump Through the Book of Proverbs (6-31)

Proverbs 6

Again, grab them by their *what*?

> A worthless person, a wicked man is the one who walks with a perverse mouth.
> Who winks with his eyes, who signals with his feet, who points with his fingers;
> Who *with* perversity in his heart continually devises evil, who spreads strife. (Proverbs 6:12–14)

Reminds me of Donald Trump! Verses 13 and 14 bring QAnon to mind; the QAnon devotees would look closely at Trump's movements while he spoke to identify these physical signals and interpret his gestures in relation to their conspiracy theories.

Every Christian who supports Trump should highlight the following verses because they are so important to think about:

> There are six things which the LORD hates,
> yes, seven which are an abomination to Him:
> Haughty eyes, a lying tongue, and hands
> that shed innocent blood,
> A heart that devises wicked plans, feet that
> run rapidly to evil,
> A false witness who utters lies, and one who
> spreads strife among brothers. (6:16–19)

Remember, if these traits are an abomination to God, then he considers them with hatred or disgust. The word *haughty* is not commonly used these days, but it means arrogantly superior and disdainful—one of Donald Trump's most pervasive traits. And Trump's lying tongue is *the* most significant trait he uses to spread strife in our country. His "Big Steal" became his "Big Lie." I often have wondered why Trump admires Vladimir Putin so much; besides Putin's control over vast amounts of wealth, his ability to manipulate truth appears to be one of the main reasons. The Russian people know their leaders lie; it is part of their culture's governance to maintain its power, and keeps any opposition off balance because no one knows what to believe. This tactic goes all the way back to Genesis 3 when the serpent tricked Eve and Adam into believing his lie instead of God's truth.

This was why Russia used cyber warfare to sow lies in our social media, undermining knowledge and truth in our elections. Putin is delighted with how well it worked, and when he denied it ever happened, Donald Trump became his corroborator, undermining our intelligence agencies by saying, "They said they think it's Russia. I have President Putin; he just said it's not Russia," adding, "I will say this: I don't see any reason why it would be."

God also hates hands that shed innocent blood (verse 17), so what of those who died as a result of the Capitol insurrection on January 6, 2021, or the innocents who died because of people believing Trump's misinformation about the COVID pandemic?

Trump's plan to foment insurrection at the Capitol on January 6, 2021, was extremely wicked (verse 18). Trump's shoving the prime minister of Montenegro out of his way so he could preen for the cameras at a NATO conference reminds me of the second part of this verse, "feet that run rapidly to evil." And Trump's record of lies and spreading strife (verse 19) are a simple fact; there is no shortage of evidence.

The loving-kindness and truth promoted in God's word creates a foundation of powerful unity that has blessed the US. However, as Jesus tell us about the devil in John 8:44, **"Whenever he tells a lie, he speaks from his own nature, because he is a liar and the father of lies."** Is it any wonder that the Lord hates a lying tongue?

These verses, Proverbs 6:16–19, are a clear indicator of God's lack of support for Donald Trump; the traits described are some of Trump's strongest traits, and yet they are what God hates, according to His word.

Proverbs 7

This chapter is mostly warnings against adultery.

Proverbs 8

Proverbs 8:13 certainly shows the Lord does not favor Trump:

> The fear of the LORD is to hate evil; pride and arrogance and the evil way and the perverted mouth, I hate.

The opposite is obvious, because in several other verses, wisdom is described as the fear of the Lord. Trump's pride and arrogance seem to spread to those who support him. Truth and loving-kindness are the opposite of pride and arrogance, and both truth and loving-kindness are lacking in Trump and most of his most ardent supporters I have observed.

> Heed instruction and be wise, and do not neglect *it*. (Proverbs 8:33)

Remember, Trump disdains instruction; he lacks the patience for it, and is so full of pride he believes that following his instincts is a better than the counsel of others.

"But he who sins against me injures himself;
all those who hate me love death." (8:36)

In Old English, *sin* meant "to miss the mark." Despite his claim of "great and unmatched wisdom," Trump obviously misses the mark with wisdom; only a fool would make the claims he has made.

Proverbs 9

Many tweets and debates showed how true Proverbs 9:7–8 is for Trump's behavior:

> He who corrects a scoffer gets dishonor for himself, and he who reproves a wicked man *gets* insults for himself.
>
> Do not reprove a scoffer, or he will hate you, reprove a wise man and he will love you.

Trump's response to those who reproved him was usually hateful disdain.

> Give *instruction* to a wise man and he will be still wiser, teach a righteous man and he will increase *his* learning. (9:9)

Remember that Trump does not seek instruction but instead prefers to rely on his instincts. Righteousness is not in those who are proud, arrogant, and insolent, as Trump is.

> The fear of the LORD is the beginning of wisdom, and the knowledge of the Holy One is understanding. (9:10)

I don't believe Donald Trump would act as he does if he understood the Holy One.

> If you are wise, you are wise for yourself, and if you scoff, you alone will bear it. (9:12)

If you don't think Trump is a scoffer, you haven't been paying attention, or maybe I should say what a scoffer is: one who speaks in a scornful, mocking, or derisive way. Watching Trump in his rallies or the 2016 Republican presidential debates shows that he is a great example of a scoffer. The Bible doesn't present scoffers in a good light.

Proverbs 10

Trump and the mob he incited to attack the Capitol validates my selection of Proverbs 10:6:

> Blessings are on the head of the righteous, but the mouth of the wicked conceals violence.

Those evil, violent people who claim righteousness are disciples of Trump, not Jesus. They did his will, not God's.

> The memory of the righteous is blessed, but
> the name of the wicked will rot. (10:7)

The videos of Trump's deceitful and undignified behaviors will be there to prove his wickedness to generations to come.

> The wise of heart will receive commands,
> but a babbling fool will be ruined. (10:8)

Trump's babbling at his rallies will also be there for posterity.

> He who walks in integrity walks securely,
> but he who perverts his ways will be found
> out. (10:9)

Posterity finds out who was perverted in history when the perverse one is no longer alive to deceitfully claim his innocence.

> He who winks the eye causes trouble, and a
> babbling fool will be ruined. (10:10)

Trump's babbling works fine at his rallies but hurt him in the presidential debates.

The mouth of the righteous is a fountain of
life, but the mouth of the wicked conceals
violence. (10:11)

Trump's rally on January 6, 2021, before the Capitol
siege by his followers, bears this out. His associates and
followers amplified his messages of violence, which can
found in the transcript of his speech at the following link:
https://www.npr.org/2021/02/10/966396848/read-trumps-
jan-6-speech-a-key-part-of-impeachment-trial.

Hatred stirs up strife, but love covers all
transgressions. (10:12)

The bitter hatred seen in so many Trump supporters
is the foundation of his divisiveness. However, most of
the time the deceived Trump supporters accuse their
opponents of doing exactly what they themselves are
doing; they often claim that the real problem is the hate
that Trump's opponents have for him. This claim was
a major part of the defense in both his impeachments.
However, we must keep in mind Proverbs 6:16, which tells
us what God hates: the arrogance, lies, moving rapidly to
evil, spreading strife among brothers. However, the love
Trump supporters have for him blinds their eyes to all his
transgressions.

Wise men store up knowledge, but with the
mouth of the foolish, ruin is at hand. (10:14)

George Washington's Farewell Address is stored-up knowledge; Trump speaks with the "mouth of the foolish."

The wages of the righteous is life, the income
of the wicked, punishment. (10:16)

Those senators who refused to hold Donald Trump accountable during the impeachment trials were supporting wickedness.

He is *on* the path of life who heeds instruction,
but he who ignores reproof goes astray. (10:17)

Trump has a tendency to "double down" when he is reproved.

He who conceals hatred *has* lying lips, and
he who spreads slander is a fool. (10:18)

Isn't there ample evidence in recordings of his rallies and in his tweets that Donald Trump was the most slanderous US president in history?

When there are many words, transgression
is unavoidable, but he who restrains his lips
is wise. (10:19)

Trump's rally and debate behaviors show the truth in this verse, even though he claims wisdom unmatched. According to scripture, Trump is obviously not wise, and he certainly had trouble restraining his lips when he debated Joe Biden.

> Doing wickedness is like sport to a fool, and *so is* wisdom to a man of understanding. (10:23)

Trump appears to enjoy spreading slander, strife, and divisiveness.

> What the wicked fears will come upon him, but the desire of the righteous will be granted. (10:24)

The election of 2020 and its aftermath will bear this out.

> When the whirlwind passes, the wicked is no more, but the righteous has an everlasting foundation. (10:25)

The righteousness of our blessed founding fathers and their writings are still standing; not so will it be with Trump.

> The hope of the righteous is gladness, but the expectation of the wicked perishes. (10:28)

Trump expected that the many legal challenges to the 2020 election would go his way, but his expectations perished.

> The way of the LORD is a stronghold to the upright, but ruin to the workers of iniquity. (10:29)

The rise of the religious left (i.e., Senator Warnock) brings gladness to many who heed the word of God.

> The lips of the righteous bring forth what is acceptable, but the mouth of the wicked what is perverted. (10:32)

Once again Trump's quote about grabbing women by their genitals comes to mind.

Proverbs 11

This chapter presents the contrasts between the upright and the wicked.

Trump's pride is well known:

> When pride comes, then comes dishonor, but with the humble is wisdom. (Proverbs 11:2)

His dishonor of being impeached *twice* is greater than any other president in the history of our great nation.

The integrity of the upright will guide them,
but the crookedness of the treacherous will
destroy them. (11:3)

The failure of Trump's many suits in court to overturn the 2020 election were just the beginning of his failures.

The righteousness of the blameless will
smooth his way, but the wicked will fall by
his own wickedness. (11:5)

Trump's term certainly wasn't smooth, and it was his wickedness that brought out a record number of voters to defeat him in 2020.

The righteousness of the upright will deliver
them, but the treacherous will be caught by
their own greed. (11:6)

It would be interesting to see how Trump's taxes connect with this proverb.

With *his* mouth the godless man destroys
his neighbor, but through knowledge the
righteous will be delivered. (11:9)

Trump's vindictive slurs toward others that did not praise him are many, and his practice of relying on his "instincts" instead of knowledge certainly didn't deliver him.

> By the blessing of the upright a city is exalted,
> but by the mouth of the wicked it is torn
> down. (11:11)

The Capitol insurrection of January 6, 2021.

> Where there is no guidance the people fall,
> but in abundance of counselors there is
> victory. (11:14)

The revolving door of those chosen by Trump to guide him resulted from his refusal to accept their counsel, relying on his instincts instead. The counselors who left were replaced with advisors who told Trump what he wanted to hear instead of giving good guidance. The word *victory* here can be translated more literally as "deliverance," but if you don't listen to your counselors, how can you be delivered? Trump's lack of victory in the 2020 election was the outcome.

> A gracious woman attains honor, and
> ruthless men attain riches. (11:16)

Does a gracious woman, especially a First Lady, appear before the media wearing "I really don't care, do you?" emblazoned on the back of her coat? Trump did attain riches—through his many bankruptcies, his ruthless deception, and legal battles.

> The wicked earns deceptive wages, but he who
> sows righteousness *gets* a true reward. (11:18)

Trump's deceived base is often called on to help by giving him money to "Stop the steal" or carry out other deceptions. When the fine print is read, it becomes clear that he uses the donations as he pleases. The "Trump Card" and his hawking a football with his signature are just other ways fleecing of his flock.

> The perverse in heart are an abomination to
> the LORD, but the blameless in *their* walk are
> His delight. (11:20)

With Trump's quotes about beautiful women, of "grab 'em by the ——," he is obviously perverse, and no one can truthfully claim he is blameless in his walk.

> *As* a ring of gold in a swine's snout so is a
> beautiful woman who lacks discretion. (11:22)

Discretion here can be described more literally as "taste." See above, Proverbs 11:16.

The desire of the righteous is only good,
but the expectation of the wicked is wrath.
(11:23)

Trump's vindictiveness toward those who disagree
with him, like calling women "dogs" and disdainfully
mocking the disabled, comes to mind.

He who diligently seeks good seeks favor, but
he who seeks evil, evil will come to him. (11:27)

I think the reader can see that this is what is happening
to Trump.

He who trusts in his riches will fall, but the
righteous will flourish like the green leaf. (11:28)

"How have the mighty fallen!" (2 Samuel 1:19).

Proverbs 12

The word *discipline* in the opening verse of Proverbs,
chapter 12, can be translated also as "instruction." Trump
certainly doesn't love instruction and would rather rely on
his instincts.

Whoever loves discipline loves knowledge,
but he who hates reproof is stupid. (Proverbs
12:1)

It is obvious that Trump hates to be reproved; similar to other authoritarian regimes in modern history, he referred to the media who did reprove him as "enemies of the people" and did all he could to undermine them.

> A man will not be established by wickedness, but the root of the righteous will not be moved. (12:3)

Thank God, Trump wasn't established.

> The thoughts of the righteous are just, but the counsels of the wicked are deceitful. (12:5)

One of Trump's strongest traits is his deceitfulness.

> The words of the wicked lie in wait for blood, but the mouth of the upright will deliver them. (12:6)

This brings to mind the words and slogans of the Capitol insurrectionists, in contrast to the language the Capitol police used while testifying in the hearings.

> A man will be praised according to his insight, but one of perverse mind will be despised. (12:8)

"Grab 'em by their ——"

The wicked man desires the booty of evil men, but the root of the righteous yields *fruit*. (12:12)

Trump's admiration of Putin's power through deceit and wealth?

An evil man is ensnared by the transgression of his lips, but the righteous will escape from trouble. (12:13)

No president in the history of our nation has been impeached twice!

The way of a fool is right in his own eyes, but a wise man is he who listens to counsel. (12:15)

How many times did we hear from Trump himself how great he was? Also his insistence that he only needed to rely on "my instincts" rather than counsel.

A fool's anger is known at once, but a prudent man conceals dishonor. (12:16)

Trump is well known for his rants against those who dishonor him.

He who speaks truth tells what is right, but a false witness, deceit. (12:17)

No US president in history has been recorded as telling more lies than Donald Trump.

> There is one who speaks rashly like the thrusts of a sword, but the tongue of the wise brings healing. (12:18)

Trump's rants and ramblings on stage are great evidence of this.

> Truthful lips will be established forever, but a lying tongue is only for a moment. (12:19)

Trump had more of those moments than any other president.

> Deceit is in the heart of those who devise evil, but counselors of peace have joy. (12:20)

Trump is much better known for his deceitful ways than his peaceful ways.

> Lying lips are an abomination to the LORD, but those who deal faithfully are His delight. (12:22)

If lies indicate an abomination to the Lord, than Trump is the most abominable president in US history. It is another proverb that indicates he is an abomination!

> A prudent man conceals knowledge, but the heart of fools proclaims folly. (12:23)

COVID-19 will "just go away"?

> The righteous is a guide to his neighbor, but the way of the wicked leads them astray. (12:26)

It is incredible that such a wicked abomination as Trump could lead our nation so far astray, but world history brings to mind others who have been even more wicked. Thank God our Constitution was able to prevent Trump from turning our democracy into his autocracy.

Proverbs 13

Trump's encouragement of the attack on our Capitol as the members of Congress were performing their duties to transition the power of the presidency to the winner of the election brings to mind Proverbs 13:2:

> From the fruit of a man's mouth he enjoys good,
> but the desire of the treacherous is violence.

Also, Trump is drawn to attend violent entertainment like the Ultimate Fighting Challenge. Just saying.

The one who guards his mouth preserves his
life; the one who opens wide his lips comes
to ruin. (13:3)

Trump's inability to control his mouth is surely his
ruin, but in a way it is the Lord's blessing that he is so
arrogant, insolent, loudmouthed, and deceitful—it clearly
shows he is not what God wants for our nation.

Through insolence comes nothing but
strife, but wisdom is with those who receive
counsel. (13:10)

Insolence is one of Trump's strongest traits, and here it
is contrasted with wisdom, his absence of which is shown
by his disdain for counsel and trusting his instincts instead.

There is a way which seems right to a man,
but its end is the way of death. (13:12)

How many of the almost one million American deaths
from the COVID pandemic came from believing Trump's
lies that COVID was no worse than the flu or would go
away by summer?

Every prudent man acts with knowledge,
but a fool displays folly. (13:16)

The way Donald Trump handled the COVID pandemic
is a good connection to make with this proverb. The

word *displays* can be taken literally to mean "spreads out." Trump's folly spread as he led his deceived base to a disdain for science, factual data, and research related to the pandemic, possibly leading to tens of thousands of their deaths. I was amazed at the folly of his followers as I witnessed their behavior at his rallies, the January 6 insurrection in 2021, and especially the extreme folly of QAnon supporters.

> A wicked messenger falls into adversity, but
> a faithful envoy brings healing. (13:17)

Trump's wickedness has led to the divisive adversity our country is currently suffering from.

> He who walks with wise men will be wise,
> but the companion of fools will suffer harm.
> (13:20)

Part of the reason there was so much turnover among Trump's advisors and the Cabinet is that any wisdom or wise experience brought into his administration was so often ignored. This verse also brings to mind his honoring the ilk of Rush Limbaugh, pardoning many criminals, and bringing in inexperienced advisors that aligned with his "instincts."

Proverbs 14

This chapter is more of the contrast between the upright and the wicked.

Lying appears to be second nature with Trump. There are websites that that daily counted the lies he told in office.

> A trustworthy witness will not lie, but a false witness utters lies. (Proverbs 14:5)

Some of Trump's closest allies were convicted of false witness; his pardon of them does not remove their guilt— it just pardons their sentence.

> A scoffer seeks wisdom and *finds* none, but knowledge is easy to one who has understanding. (14:6)

This verse makes it clear that when a great scoffer like Trump still claims he has "great and unmatched wisdom," it is clearly a lie, and knowledge is denied to one who does not understand what is good and what is evil. Trump is still lying about the 2020 election, which in and of itself is not such a big deal—at best, he is delusional; at worst, deceitful. Regardless of which, the reality is that millions of his misled supporters believe him. Many claim to be Christians and don't realize that their witness for Christ is discounted by their following a man who claims to follow God but won't obey His word. It is far more important to obey the commands of Jesus than to follow such a false prophet.

> Leave the presence of a fool, or you will not
> discern words of knowledge. (14:7)

Remember the verse about a fool being one that claims to be wise? Trump claimed unmatched wisdom!

> The wisdom of the sensible is to understand
> his way, but the foolishness of fools is deceit.
> (14:8)

Deceit appears to be Trump's natural inclination. His downplaying the seriousness of the COVID pandemic was very unwise and deceitful.

> There is a way *which seems* right to a person,
> but its end is the way of death. (14:12)

Following a liar is how our nation often led the world in cases and deaths from the COVID pandemic. It seemed right to many to believe President Trump when he said it was "under control" or that it would be over by summer.

> The naive believes everything, but the
> sensible man considers his steps. (14:15)

Thank God for those Christians who are realizing that He would not want them to follow someone who acts in ways that God says He hates.

> A wise man is cautious and turns away from evil, but a fool is arrogant and careless. (14:16)

It amazes me how so many of Trump's followers adopt his behaviors, especially his pride, arrogance, insolence, and lack of discretion.

> A quick-tempered man acts foolishly, and a man of evil devices is hated. (14:17)

Perhaps this is the basis for all those "Trump-haters" his followers refer to.

> The naive inherit foolishness, but the sensible are crowned with knowledge. (14:18)

Oh, that the naïve would become sensible! It can be done through God's word.

> Will they not go astray who devise evil? But kindness and truth *will be to* those who devise good. (14:22)

This verse brings to mind the many Trumpublican legislators that defend Trump's deceit and then devise ways to prevent people from voting by devious means, while claiming they are upholding truth in the voting process.

> The crown of the wise is their riches, but the
> folly of fools is foolishness. (14:24)

It is true that wisdom can lead to riches, but some, like Trump, get their riches from their parents, and their foolishness leads to bankruptcy. But six times? That seems like a lot of folly.

> A truthful witness saves lives, but he who
> utters lies is treacherous. (14:25)

This word *utters* literally means "breathes out." Lying is like breathing to Trump; it is part of his nature. The January attack on the Capitol was treacherous indeed!

> He who is slow to anger has great
> understanding, but he who is quick-tempered
> exalts folly (14:29)

Quick-tempered can be translated more literally as "short of spirit."

> He who oppresses the poor taunts his Maker,
> but he who is gracious to the needy honors
> Him. (14:31)

This is another verse that brings to mind the legislators who are making laws that make it harder for the poor and needy to vote in the democracy that God has blessed us with here in the United States of America! Let's pray to God our Supreme Court can understand and discern their role in protecting our fellow Americans' right to vote.

Many of the poor in our nation still suffer from the "previous condition of servitude" of their ancestors—something the Fifteenth Amendment sought to protect them from. Such generational poverty requires the intervention of education to break the cycle of suppressing their inability to communicate and think at a higher level. This can be a gracious way to provide access to higher-paying employment.

> The wicked is thrust down by his wrongdoing, but the righteous has a refuge when he dies. (14:32)

The 2020 election thrust Trump down, yet he still lies about it.

> Wisdom rests in the heart of one who has understanding, but in the hearts of fools it is made known. (14:33)

Again, as we have seen in God's word, Trump's boasting about his "unmatched wisdom" makes him a fool.

Righteousness exalts a nation, but sin is a disgrace to *any* people. (14:34)

The righteousness of the United States is its most powerful influence on the rest of the world; it leads to God being able to bless us in ways other nations would love to be blessed. But when our leaders sin, our enemies highlight their sin to the rest of the world. Russia's Putin is delighted with the disgrace the US has faced as Trump lied his way through his term as president. Putin knows democratic republics thrive on truth and loving-kindness—just what Jesus exemplifies. Putin was delighted with Trump's lying and vindictiveness, because that is how democracy can be weakened.

Proverbs 15

The contrast of the upright and the wicked continues in this chapter.

In the battle against COVID, I never expected Trump would find the knowledge of scientists to be unacceptable but then offer suggestions like ingesting disinfectants.

The tongue of the wise makes knowledge acceptable, but the mouth of fools spouts folly. (Proverbs 15:2)

COVID would disappear?

A soothing tongue is a tree of life, but perversion in it crushes the spirit. (15:4)

It is hard on the people's spirit when a leader demonstrates perversion.

The lips of the wise spread knowledge, but the hearts of fools are not so. (15:7)

Trump's COVID response certainly wasn't based on knowledge.

The way of the wicked is an abomination to the LORD, but He loves one who pursues righteousness. (15:9)

As we have seen in other verses of Proverbs, Trump ways are an abomination.

A scoffer does not love one who reproves him, he will not go to the wise. (15:12)

The Republicans who held Trump accountable were scoffed at by Trump. Scores of judges reviewing the suits filed by Trump and his supporters were also scoffed at by Trump, even the US Supreme Court.

The mind of the intelligent seeks knowledge, but the mouth of fools feeds on folly. (15:14)

Trump got much of what knowledge he had from watching the folly of media like Fox News.

> A hot-tempered man stirs up strife, but the slow to anger calms a dispute. (15:18)

Stirring up strife is one of Trump's greatest traits; it's no wonder the US is so ridden with strife after four years of his insolent scoffing and lies.

> Folly is joy to him who lacks sense, but a man of understanding walks straight. (15:21)

It is amazing how many Bible verses say not to turn to the right or to the left.

> Without consultation, plans are frustrated, but with many counselors they succeed. (15:22)

As discussed in Bob Woodward's writing, based on recorded interviews, Trump preferred his "instincts" over expert advice or research.

> Evil plans are an abomination to the LORD, but pleasant words are pure. (15:26)

Trump certainly makes evil plans.

The heart of the righteous ponders how to answer, but the mouth of the wicked pours out evil things. (15:28)

If you listen to Trump's response to questions, he almost never ponders how to answer. He just keeps rambling and then often lies to make himself appear to be doing a better job than anyone else in history.

He whose ear listens to the life-giving reproof will dwell among the wise. (15:31)

Trump himself says he trust his instincts before the counsel of others; those who offer reproof receive scorn in return.

The fear of the LORD is the instruction for wisdom, and before honor *comes* humility. (15:33)

Trump appears to put his honor before humility.

Proverbs 16

Is Trump our golden calf?

The Lord has made everything for its own purpose, even the wicked for the day of evil. (Proverbs 16:4)

Were the wicked leaders who led the nation of Israel to its destruction all part of the plan to punish them for following idols instead of the Lord?

> Everyone who is proud in heart is an abomination to the Lord; be assured, he will not go unpunished. (16:5)

Trump's pride is one of his strongest traits, yet God's word says that makes him an abomination that will not go unpunished. How can a follower of Christ also follow and adore an abomination?

> By lovingkindness and truth iniquity is atoned for, and by the fear of the Lord one keeps away from evil. (16:6)

Never forget God's greatest example of loving-kindness and truth: Jesus atoning for our sins through His death on the cross so we could be with Him. This gives everyone redemption, and those who accept this gift also receive salvation leading to sanctification. The fear of the Lord is based on not taking that for granted and revering His almighty power, which is wild beyond our imagination.

> When a man's ways are pleasing to the Lord, He makes even his enemies to be at peace with him. (16:7)

This is a truly convicting verse of scripture! Trump certainly isn't at peace with his enemies, and no one could truly say he is.

> Better is a little with righteousness than great income with injustice. (16:8)

The economy of a country is not more important than the integrity of its principles.

> The mind of man plans his way, but the Lord directs his steps. (16:9)

This direction by the Lord doesn't always lead to meeting the man's desired outcome.

> How much better it is to get wisdom than gold! And to get understanding is to be chosen above silver. (16:16)

Trump certainly doesn't feel he needs more wisdom; according to him, his is "great and unmatched"!

> Pride *goes* before destruction, and a haughty spirit before stumbling. (16:18)

There is no doubt that Trump will become an example of this truth in God's word.

> It is better to be humble in spirit with the
> lowly than to divide the spoil with the proud.
> (16:19)

For his own sake, I pray that Trump could learn how true this is.

> He who gives attention to the word will find
> good, and blessed is he who trusts in the
> Lord. (16:20)

I have found this to be an undeniable fact in my life and in others' too.

> Understanding is a fountain of life to one
> who has it, but the discipline of fools is folly.
> (16:22)

Trump's lack of understanding and his folly are his undoing, and he leads his followers there. This is how the US has become the **"divided house"** that Jesus spoke of in Matthew 12:25, Mark 3:25, and Luke 11:17.

> There is a way *which seems* right to a man,
> but its end is the way of death. (Proverbs
> 16:25)

This reminds me of those who stormed our Capitol to prevent our democracy's transfer of power from Trump.

In a twisted way, they believe they are righteous, but the outcome for too many people was death. This could also apply to Trump's approach to the COVID pandemic.

> A worthless man digs up evil, while his words are like scorching fire. (16:27)

Talk about scorching fire! Review on the internet what Trump told his supporters when he said to "fight like ——" before they stormed the Capitol building.

> A perverse man spreads strife, and a slanderer separates intimate friends. (16:28)

So many of those misled by Trump ignore his comments (such as grabbing women by their genitals), but their very close friends have not forgotten his proud perversity, for which he has never asked forgiveness; it leads to strife among many friends and family members.

> A man of violence entices his neighbor and leads him in a way that is not good. (16:29)

Another proverb related to the insurrection of January 6, 2021, at our Capitol building.

> He who winks his eyes *does so* to devise perverse things; He who compresses his lips brings evil to pass. (16:30)

If you don't believe this applies to Trump, notice how often he compresses his lips.

> A gray head is a crown of glory; it is found in the way of righteousness. (16:31)

No gray hair on Trump!

> He who is slow to anger is better than the mighty, and he who rules his spirit, than he who captures a city. (16:32)

Trump obviously is not slow to anger and does not rule his spirit.

Proverbs 17

Trump gave more credence to Vladimir Putin (a frequent liar) than to our own intelligence agencies. It was literally unbelievable when he refuted claims of Russian interference in the 2016 US elections because Putin denied it. Even more incredible is Trump's praising Putin for invading Ukraine as "genius"!

> An evildoer listens to wicked lips; a liar pays attention to a destructive tongue. (Proverbs 17:4)

Trump had a mentor by the name of Roy Cohn, who became well known as a young chief counsel to Senator Joe McCarthy in the disgraceful United States Army hearings during the 1950s. One of his famous quotes was "I don't want to know what the law is, I want to know who the judge is." He taught Trump to never admit to any wrongdoing or defeat. There are many documentaries about Cohn. He was eventually disbarred in New York and died of AIDS.

> The beginning of strife is *like* letting out water, so abandon the quarrel before it breaks out. (17:14)

Trump learned from his mentor Roy Cohn to always counterattack and hit back harder. His tweets were often a response to someone saying something that might make him look bad. It appears Trump also learned Cohn's preference for looking tanned.

> He who justifies the wicked and he who condemns the righteous, both of them alike are an abomination to the Lord. (17:15)

Trump's rewards and pardons of friends and criminals, while condemning the righteous who reproved him, can be seen here. According to God's word, the Donald is clearly an abomination.

Why is there a price in the hand of a fool to
buy wisdom, when he has no sense? (17:16)

Trump doesn't have the sense to spend time or money
on acquiring wisdom; he believes following his instincts
is the best path.

He who has a crooked mind finds no good,
and he who is perverted in his language falls
into evil. (17:20)

Trump swears and scoffs with derision more than any
president I have ever heard.

A wicked man receives a bribe from the
bosom to pervert the ways of justice. (17:23)

Trump's call to the Department of Justice to tell them
to send out a message describing the 2020 election as
"corruption" comes to mind here.

He who restrains his words has knowledge,
and he who has a cool spirit is a man of
understanding. (17:27)

Another of Trump's traits is showing his lack of
restraint or understanding by what he says, indicating that
he is more of a hot head than a cool spirit.

Proverbs 18

Trump proudly lays claim to outsider status in politics and being guided by his instincts rather than the sound wisdom of counsel.

> He who separates himself seeks his own desire, he quarrels against all sound wisdom. A fool does not delight in understanding, but only in revealing his own mind. (Proverbs 1–2)

Verse 2 reminds me again of Trump and his preference for relying on his instincts instead of advice from experts in a field.

> When a wicked man comes, contempt also comes, and with dishonor *comes* scorn. (18:3)

This verse reminds me of many of Trump's tweets, which often showered contempt, dishonor, and scorn on those who publicly disagreed with him.

> To show partiality to the wicked is not good, *nor* to thrust aside the righteous in judgment. (18:5)

This proverb is good to link to Trump's pardoning of the criminals who lied for him and awarding medals to those who praise him. What also comes to mind is the behavior of Trump's congressional supporters during the impeachment trials; several witnesses who were simply telling the truth were castigated for doing so.

> A fool's lips bring strife, and his mouth calls for blows. (18:6)

This is another proverb that applies to Trump's rally leading up to the insurrection at the Capitol on January 6, where his crowd chanted "Fight for Trump."

> A fool's mouth is his ruin, and his lips are the snare of his soul. (18:7)

Many things Trump said are coming back as evidence against him, like the snare of being impeached twice.

> A rich man's wealth is his strong city, and like a high wall in his own imagination. (18:11)

This fuels Trump's litigious pattern of behavior as he uses the courts to dissuade others from seeking retribution for his deceitful practices.

> Before destruction the heart of a person is haughty, but humility *goes* before honor. (18:12)

It will be interesting to see whether Trump ever realizes the power of humility to bring him honor.

> The mind of the prudent acquires knowledge,
> and the ear of the wise seeks knowledge.
> (18:15)

According to his own words and the words of those in his Cabinet, Trump does not seek knowledge (he trusts his instincts) except by listening to those who praise him and tell him what he wants to hear, such as right-wing talk-show hosts and pundits.

> With the fruit of a man's mouth his stomach
> will be satisfied; he will be satisfied *with* the
> product of his lips. (18:20)

This has been very true for Donald Trump; his ability to use words to get his way has been a very strong behavioral trait. A con man must be able to speak well.

> Death and life are in the power of the
> tongue, and those who love it will eat its
> fruit. (18:21)

This applies to good, but also to evil. There are many more proverbs that address speaking well while also knowing when not to speak.

The poor man utters supplications, but the
rich man answers roughly. (18:23)

Rough answers are also a strong trait of Trump's.

Proverbs 19

This chapter highlights our Lord's emphasis on truth and
loving-kindness—traits where Trump comes up short.

Better is a poor man who walks in his
integrity than he who is perverse in speech
and is a fool. (Proverbs 19:1)

However, perverse speech appeals to fools of a perverse
mind.

A false witness will not go unpunished, and
he who tells lies will not escape. (19:5)

One of Trump's most distinguishing traits is his lying.
As a developer, he was a well-known liar and often cheated
others out of money he owed them. One example of his
being a false witness was his claim that Barack Obama was
not born in the United States, making him unqualified
to be president, claiming falsely that Obama was born in
Kenya.

A false witness will not go unpunished, and
he who tells lies will perish. (19:9)

As I write, Trump's lies to avoid paying taxes appear to
be catching up with him.

A man's discretion makes him slow to anger,
and it is his glory to overlook a transgression.
(19:11)

Trump's anger and vindictiveness are two of his
stronger traits.

Listen to counsel and accept discipline, that
you may be wise the rest of your days. (19:20)

It was well known, especially by his advisors, that
Trump preferred to rely on his own instincts or those who
often agreed with him. *Discipline* in this verse, as noted
previously, can also be translated as "instruction."

What is desirable in a man is his kindness, and
it is better to be a poor man than a liar. (19:22)

God's word is pretty clear here. Trump is short on
kindness, and being a liar is one of his strongest traits.

A rascally witness makes a mockery of
justice, and the mouth of the wicked spreads
iniquity. (19:28)

Trump's incessant lies truly make him a rascally witness, and his choosing judges to do his bidding, as if they owed *him* loyalty, was certainly a mockery of justice. His comments related to the Supreme Court not siding with him on lawsuits to overturn the election he lost was a historic mockery that spread to the riot at the Capitol after he stirred his supporters—an infamous example of spreading iniquity. The mockery of justice was also evident in many of the pardons Trump doled out to those more loyal to him than to justice in our nation, even removing attorneys general who wouldn't subvert the law at Trump's whim. The callous indifference of many of Trump's supporters toward his dismantling of the Department of Justice by filling it with those loyal to his bidding also brings to mind Jesus describing the end times in Matthew 24:12: **"Because lawlessness is increased most people's love will grow cold."**

Judgments are prepared for scoffers, and
blows for the back of fools. (19:29)

The judgments denying scores of Trump's suits to overturn election results, and Trump's habit of scoffing obviously come together here.

Proverbs 20

Trump appears to be drawn to strife and quarreling; it is like a reflex action for him.

Keeping away from strife is an honor for a
man, but any fool will quarrel. (Proverbs
20:3)

Considering this verse, I am puzzled by those Christian
Trump supporters who admire him as a "fighter."

Many a man proclaims his own loyalty, but
who can find a trustworthy man? (20:6)

Trump primarily proclaims loyalty to himself and
shows a pattern of getting rid of any of his advisors who
appear not to put loyalty to him above all else.

There is gold, and an abundance of jewels;
but the lips of knowledge are a more precious
thing. (20:15)

Trump's love of gold is common knowledge, and so
is his aversion to gaining knowledge through reading or
listening to his advisors.

Prepare plans by consultation, and make
war by wise guidance. (20:18)

Trump follows his "instincts" rather than this proverb.
In his role as Commander in Chief, Trump refused to
depend on wise guidance for war. As a result, the Chairman
of the Joint Chiefs of Staff, General Mark Milley, let China

know that Trump's talk of war with China was not to be taken seriously. When this was revealed, it outraged Trump supporters, but relieved others who were worried Trump would start a war to justify not transferring power after he lost the 2020 presidential election.

> The glory of young men is their strength,
> and the honor of old men is their gray hair.
> (20:29)

I wonder if this honor (see also 16:31) belongs to old men like Trump who dye their hair; it doesn't appear to be so in his case.

Proverbs 21

Trump certainly has these traits:

> Haughty eyes and a proud heart, the lamp of
> the wicked is sin. (Proverbs 21:4)

Those who know that God hates these traits can see that Trump emanates sin and not the fruits of the Spirit.

> The acquisition of treasures by a lying tongue
> is a fleeting vapor, the pursuit of death. (21:6)

Six bankruptcies even after receiving hundreds of millions from his father?

The violence of the wicked will drag them
away, because they refuse to act with justice.
(21:7)

The Lafayette Square riots, his urging those at his rally to
"fight" on January 6, 2021, and their corresponding attack
on the Capitol, all come to mind here. Trump insisted that
Vice President Pence decertify the 2020 election results
instead of following what the US Constitution said he must
do, and he filed many lawsuits to overturn those results—
blatant refusals to act with justice!

When the scoffer is punished, the naive
becomes wise; but when the wise is
instructed, he receives knowledge. (21:11)

Trump is neither naïve nor wise, as is evident from his
lack of humility and refusal to face the truth that he lost
the 2020 election. Considering his claims that he won that
election in a landslide, at best he is delusional, and at the
worst he is a liar. Hopefully, Trump's naïve followers will
become wise as they see him losing in our courts, with so
many legal decisions going against him.

The exercise of justice is joy for the righteous,
but is terror to the workers of iniquity. (21:15)

This verse brings to mind Trump's second impeachment
trial, when the Senate failed to reach a two-thirds majority

vote to convict him, and he was acquitted because so many Republican senators were fearful of retribution from those who approved the wickedness of the Capitol insurrection.

²² A wise man scales the city of the mighty and brings down the stronghold in which they trust.

Those bipartisan congressman involved in the congressional investigations of the Capitol insurrection are wise enough to find and uphold the truth that brings down the power of political parties to obfuscate the truth.

He who guards his mouth and his tongue,
guards his soul from troubles. (21:23)

Trump doesn't appear to be able to do this well at all. His rambling often leads to foolishness.

"Proud," "Haughty," "Scoffer," are his names,
who acts with insolent pride. (21:24)

God's word seems pretty clear here as a description of Donald Trump.

There is no wisdom and no understanding
and no counsel against the LORD. (21:30)

Amen!

Proverbs 22

My comments are meant only to shed light on the vast amount of scripture that appears to have amazingly clear application to Donald Trump. If my comments appear to be biased against him, then ignore them—but please consider the scripture apart from my comment. From your perspective, how does it apply?

> He who sows iniquity will reap vanity, and the rod of his fury will perish. (Proverbs 22:8)

Trump's iniquities got him ratings of media coverage; only vanity, but that was something he prized highly. His rants no longer get as much attention because he has less power to ruin the democracy of the USA. And although he won't admit it, our republic's Constitution prevented him from continuing his autocratic attempt to gain more power.

> Drive out the scoffer, and contention will go out, even strife and dishonor will cease. (22:10)

With Trump no longer president of the USA, his scoffing doesn't have as much divisive impact that it had before, and our Nation's strife and dishonor are slowly being reduced. There is more talk now of the need of our citizens to see themselves as Americans rather than democrats or republicans, conservative or liberal; our enemies are delighted by the strife creating wedges and eroding unity among our people.

> The eyes of the LORD preserve knowledge, but He overthrows the words of the treacherous man. (22:12)

It appears many of Trump's more thoughtful followers have left him due to his inciting of the 1/6/21 Capitol insurrection and his lies about his loss of the 2020 presidential election

> The mouth of an adulteress is a deep pit; he who is cursed of the LORD will fall into it. (22:14)

Trump's adulteries are no secret and he is deeper in that pit every time he lies about them.

> He who oppresses the poor to make more for himself or who gives to the rich, *will* only *come to* poverty. (22:16)

Trump's cuts for programs of those in poverty and tax cuts for the wealthy? It will be interesting to see what happens as a result of all the legal action being taken against Trump. However, as long as he can con his supporters into sending him money it will delay his poverty. It is his supporters who are so deceived they are "giving to the rich" when they send him money. Sadly, aren't they often the ones coming to poverty too?

Verses 17–21 of Proverbs 22 remind us of the importance of applying the word of God and His truth to our lives:

> Incline your ear and hear the words of the
> wise, and apply your mind to my knowledge;
> For it will be pleasant if you keep them within
> you, that they may be ready on your lips.
> So that your trust may be in the LORD, I have
> taught you today, even you.
> Have I not written to you excellent things of
> counsels and knowledge,
> To make you know the certainty of the words
> of truth that you may correctly answer him
> who sent you?

Too many in our nation have put their trust in false prophets and their idols instead of these verses.

> Do not associate with a man *given* to anger;
> or go with a hot-tempered man, or you will
> learn his ways and find a snare for yourself.
> (22:24)

Trump learned much of his behavior from Roy Cohn, the New York City attorney who was eventually disbarred for his deceitful practices. He was Trump's mentor, teaching him to hit back harder through the courts and never admit wrongdoing or defeat. Cohn also had the same fake-tan look.

Proverbs 23

Many of Trump's advisors quit because he ignored or disdained their counsel.

> Do not speak in the hearing of a fool, for
> he will despise the wisdom of your words.
> (Proverbs 23:9)

Proverbs 24

Toward the end of his term, as Trump fought to spread his lie that he won the 2020 election by a landslide, he refused to listen to many who counseled him not to tarnish his legacy by refusing to commit to a peaceful transition of power to the administration of the certified winner, Joe Biden.

> For by wise guidance you will wage war, and
> in abundance of counselors there is victory.
> (Proverbs 24:6)

Trump's defeat became more infamous as he refused wise guidance.

One who plans to do evil, men will call a
schemer. (24:8)

Trump's directions for Vice President Pence to ignore
our Constitution's directions for certifying the electoral
count, and his calls to leaders in swing states to alter the
election counts, were more of his deviously evil schemes to
keep himself in power despite losing the election.

The devising of folly is sin, and the scoffer is
an abomination to men. (24:9)

The folly Trump displayed through his misinformation
in response to the COVID pandemic was surely responsible
for untold amounts of death and suffering. Added to this
was his scoffing aimed at doctors and scientists trying to
implement precautions to prevent the spread of COVID. I
don't think anyone with credibility can deny that Trump
is a scoffer and therefore an abomination; you can't argue
with the word of God.

Deliver those who are being taken away
to death, and those who are staggering to
slaughter, Oh, hold *them* back. (24:11)

I pray that the awareness of what God's word has
shown in the book of Proverbs can prevent many from
joining those whose ignorance led them to die as a result
of following Trump.

> If you say, "See, we did not know this,"
> does He not consider *it* who weighs the
> hearts? And does He not know *it* who keeps
> your soul? And will He not render to man
> according to his work? (24:12)

Proverbs 24:11–12 added greatly to my motivation to write this book.

> For a righteous man falls seven times, and
> rises again, but the wicked stumble in *time*
> *of* calamity. (24:16)

Who can deny Trump's reaction to the COVID-19 virus was certainly a stumble!

> Do not fret because of evildoers, or be
> envious of the wicked;
> For there will be no future for the evil man;
> the lamp of the wicked will be put out.
> (24:19–20)

From the beginning of Trump's administration, I had faith that the Lord would not allow him to overcome the Constitution of the United States.

> These also are sayings of the wise. To show
> partiality in judgment is not good. (24:23)

Trump's manipulation of our nation's judicial system was "not good" and did him no good in the end.

> He who says to the wicked, "You are righteous," peoples will curse him, nations will abhor him. (24:24)

This verse reminds me of Trump's behavior toward Vladimir Putin. Trump gave more credibility to him than to the intelligence agencies of the United States! Sadly, it can also be applied to those who continue to believe Trump is righteous.

> But to those who rebuke the *wicked* will be delight, and a good blessing will come upon them. (24:25)

After seeing how Trump treated many of those who served in his Cabinet and rebuked him, it was no wonder several of them let others know of the danger his lack of leadership presented.

Proverbs 25

I pray that an awareness of what Proverbs says about those like Trump will be a blessing to all.

> Like clouds and wind without rain is a
> person who boasts of his gifts falsely.
> (Proverbs 25:14)

Trump claimed, "I alone can fix this!", but things got worse.

> Like a bad tooth and an unsteady foot is
> confidence in a treacherous person in time
> of trouble. (25:19)

This verse points to what a con man Trump is. The people of the United States put their confidence in Trump as he claimed to be a "wartime president" in response to the COVID pandemic, and the result was more dead Americans than from the wars in our nation's history.

> *Like* a trampled spring and a polluted well
> is a righteous man who gives way before the
> wicked. (25:26)

This verse makes me think of the many evangelical leaders who support Trump despite his continuous lies; but perhaps they're not righteous? I don't know; I don't believe I can judge them, but it does make me wonder.

> It is not good to eat much honey, nor is it
> glory to search out one's own glory. (25:27)

This verse explains how Trump's self-promotion only made him look foolish to those who were immune to his arrogant and deceptive bragging.

> *Like* a city that is broken into and without walls is a man who has no control over his spirit. (25:28)

This reminds me of his lack of control in the 2020 presidential debates. I am amazed at how deceit comes to him so naturally, like a deceitful spirit.

Proverbs 26

> Do not answer a fool according to his folly, or you will also be like him. (Proverbs 26:4)

This seemed to work well for Biden when he debated Trump.

> Answer a fool as his folly *deserves*, that he not be wise in his own eyes. (26:5)

This leads me to consider congressional Republicans who refused to join in Trump's deceitful schemes.

> Like a dog that returns to its vomit is a fool who repeats his folly. (26:11)

Even after being impeached twice, and losing the presidency after one term, Donald Trump is still spouting lies to continue to divide the people of this nation.

> Do you see a man wise in his own eyes?
> There is more hope for a fool than for him.
> (26:12)

Remember Trump's tweet "In my great and unmatched wisdom ..."?

> Like a madman who throws firebrands,
> arrows and death. (26:18)

It's ironic that Trump pointed out that the deaths from the January 6 Capitol insurrection shouldn't have happened, but he was the firebrand that incited it.

> So is the man who deceives his neighbor,
> and says, "Was I not joking?" (26:19)

This proverb reminds me of several times Trump said something as deceiving as "I am the chosen one" and then later claimed he was being sarcastic, or when Trump's staff often claimed he was only joking.

> For lack of wood the fire goes out, and where there is no whisperer, contention quiets down. (26:20)

Without a platform like Twitter, things have settled down some, but the whisperer Trump is still spreading strife whenever he can. Isn't it so ironic and deceitful that Trump named his social media app Truth?

> *Like* charcoal to hot embers and wood to fire,
> so is a contentious man to kindle strife. (26:21)

Unlike most presidents after they leave office, Trump keeps sniping from the sidelines, like endorsing primary candidates who support his Big Lie or making comments to derail momentum for improvement rather than helping the country.

> The words of a whisperer are like dainty morsels, and they go down into the innermost parts of the body. (26:22)

Verses 21 and 22 can be read together. The former shows what has happened, and the latter shows that even after being impeached twice and leaving office under a cloud of fomenting insurrection, Trump continues a pattern of pathological lies to stoke the fires of his misled followers' desire to return him to the power he abused. His continuing ability to con his supporters out of money is amazing.

> He who hates disguises *it* with his lips, but he lays up deceit in his heart. (26:24)

Trump's comments concerning a peaceful transition between his administration and Biden's are a good example of how his words were so different from his actions during the transition. Shortly after the January 6 insurrection, he tweeted through his deputy chief of staff for communications, Dan Scavino:

> *Even though I totally disagree with the outcome of the election, and the facts bear me out, nevertheless there will be an orderly transition on January 20th. I have always said we would continue our fight to ensure that only legal votes were counted. While this represents the end of the greatest first term in presidential history, it's only the beginning of our fight to Make America Great Again!*

Now we know the problems our National Archives are having with Trump taking classified documents to his residence in Florida.

> When he speaks graciously, do not believe him, for there are seven abominations in his heart. (26:25)

Here is a good example of Trump's gracious yet deceitful statement after the attack on the Capitol:

I know your pain. I know you're hurt. We had an election that was stolen from us. It was a landslide election and everyone knows it, especially the other side. But you have to go home now. We have to have peace. We have to have law and order. We have to respect our great people in law and order. We don't want anybody hurt. It's a very tough period of time. There's never been a time like this where such a thing happened. Where they could take it away from all of us: From me, from you, from our country. This was a fraudulent election, but we can't play into the hands of these people. We have to have peace. So, go home. We love you. You are very special. You've seen what happens. You see the way others are treated that are so bad, so evil. I know how you feel. But go home and go home in peace.

Though his hatred covers itself with guile, his wickedness will be revealed before the assembly. (26:26)

Those journalists who revealed his wickedness Trump called the "enemy of the people," but many of their reported facts eventually came out in the impeachment trials. The investigative hearings for the Capitol insurrection revealed even more wickedness.

He who digs a pit will fall into it, and he who
rolls a stone, it will come back on him. (26:27)

No president of the United States has ever been
impeached twice! Trump appears to be falling into the pit
of deceit he has dug in refusing to show his tax returns.
Could the stone rolling back on him be his incitement of
the Capitol insurrection on January 6, 2021?

A lying tongue hates those it crushes and a
flattering mouth works ruin. (26:28)

Trump's laughable "bromance" with Kim Jong Un
comes to mind in this oft repeated quote: "I was really
tough and so was he, and we would go back and forth.
And then we fell in love. No, really. He wrote me beautiful
letters."

Proverbs 27

I often wonder: does Trump actually believe his own
boasting, or is it just meant to mislead others to follow him?

Do not boast about tomorrow, for you do not
know what a day may bring forth. (Proverbs
27:1)

Trump's big, beautiful wall that Mexico was supposed

to pay for, or his claim of being a "wartime president" in his approach to the COVID pandemic, come to mind here.

> Let another praise you, and not your own
> mouth; a stranger, and not your own lips.
> (27:2)

It's apparent Trump almost agrees with this proverb when Premier Christian News (PCN) reported that he claimed to be "the chosen one." PCN now seems to have taken down the page, but an online search will produce video of the quote from the BBC, C-SPAN, and others. Amazon even has a T-shirt with humorous Trump quotes, with "I am the chosen one" on top.

> A stone is heavy and the sand weighty, but
> the provocation of a fool is heavier than both
> of them. (27:3)

Trump's comments appeared to have provoked riots across the country, in particular the ones like Lafayette Square and the Capitol insurrection.

Proverbs 28

Proverbs 28:4 brings to mind the pardons Trump dealt out according to his whims.

Those who forsake the law praise the wicked,
but those who keep the law strive with them.

But worse than that is the law-forsaken tactics of the political parties in our nation—the ones George Washington warned us about. It will be our undoing if we allow the parties to swing our country's foundation of a government based on upholding the law, to something like the Trump administration's practice of using the law to further the political aims of the president or increase the power of one political party over another.

Evil men do not understand justice, but those who seek the Lord understand all things. (28:5)

For Trump, it appears that justice was to be used for his purposes of furthering his self-centered agenda and power. But this verse is evident in the US Supreme Court's refusal to support his lies about how the 2020 election was stolen from him, even though he appointed a third of them.

Better is the poor who walks in his integrity
than he who is crooked though he be rich.
(28:6)

So many of Trump's supporters have excused his rude behavior because he is wealthy and famous.

He who turns away his ear from listening to
the law, even his prayer is an abomination.
(28:9)

It was "Proverbs in action" when Trump turned the
National Day of Prayer Breakfast in Washington into his
own political speech.

He who leads the upright astray in an evil
way will himself fall into his own pit, but the
blameless will inherit good. (28:10)

Verse 10 shows how the evil way of deceit will create a
pit for those leaders who use it, and those who don't will
benefit.

The rich man is wise in his own eyes, but the
poor who has understanding sees through
him. (28:11)

Many have followed Trump because he has branded
himself as a great businessman. They overlook his
many bankruptcies, explaining that this is what good
businessmen do. No one with true understanding would
call that good business—shrewd maybe, but not good.

When the righteous triumph, there is great
glory, but when the wicked rise, men hide
themselves. (28:12)

Toward the end of Trump's days in office, he had trouble finding legal counsel of quality to defend his lies and actions.

> He who conceals his transgressions will not prosper, but he who confesses and forsakes *them* will find compassion. (28:13)

Could Trump's refusal to ever admit his wrongdoing be the reason so many lack compassion for him?

> How blessed is the man who fears always, but he who hardens his heart will fall into calamity. (28:14)

When you fear the Lord, you don't have to fear anything else.

> A leader who is a great oppressor lacks understanding, b*ut* he who hates unjust gain will prolong his days. (28:16)

Trump's flagrant misunderstanding of climate change and reductions of environmental protections for the purpose of wealth come to mind here.

> A faithful man will abound with blessings, but he who makes haste to be rich will not go unpunished. (28:20)

Being impeached twice is certainly punishment without historical precedent. Also, as the legal inquiries into his tax returns unfold, a link to this proverb might become obvious.

> An arrogant man stirs up strife, but he who
> trusts in the Lord will prosper. (28:25)

Trump's lack of trust in the Lord will soon be evident; his bankruptcies and legal bills will not allow him to prosper. However, his supporters are still sending him money. That will come to an end as he is brought to justice and more of them come to the realization that they were conned.

> He who trusts in his own heart is a fool, but
> he who walks wisely will be delivered. (28:26)

As has been shown by several proverbs, Trump is a fool, and isn't trusting in his own instincts like trusting in his heart?

> One who gives to the poor will never lack
> *anything*, but one who shuts his eyes will
> have many curses. (28:27)

Trump has certainly hasn't been known as a champion of the poor.

> When the wicked rise, people hide
> themselves; but when they perish, the
> righteous increase. (28:28)

Our nation's president can affect the norms of behavior of our people; the mean, arrogant insolence of many of Trump's supporters is rampant in social media. It already seems to be dissipating in the first year without him as the president of our nation. When it is replaced by the loving-kindness and truth of Jesus, the righteous will increase.

Proverbs 29

It is hard for Trump supporters to understand why so many people groan at Trump's wickedness.

> When the righteous increase, the people
> rejoice, but when a wicked man rules, people
> groan. (Proverbs 29:2)

Trump's supporters are blinded to his wickedness by ignorance of what the word of God has to say about a leader with his behavioral traits.

> The righteous is concerned for the rights of
> the poor, the wicked does not understand
> *such* concern. (29:7)

Trump certainly doesn't seem concerned about addressing the reasons for the increase in the homeless in this country. His lack of support for programs concerned with the need for education to lift the generationally poor out of poverty was obvious.

> Scorners set a city aflame, but wise men turn
> away anger. (29:8)

This reminds me of the Black Lives Matter riots. Trump was incapable of turning away that anger; he made it worse by trying to create his unwise "law and order" propagandistic photo op in Lafayette Square. It backfired when some of his Cabinet publicly rebuked such an unwise display. Thank God for our military leaders who wisely saw through his ploy.

> When a wise man has a controversy with a
> foolish man, the foolish man either rages or
> laughs, and there is no rest. (29:9)

This was shown in debates that Trump participated in.

> A fool always loses his temper, but a wise
> man holds it back. (29:11)

Again the 2020 debates come to mind, when Trump couldn't restrain his impulsive mouth.

> If a ruler pays attention to falsehood, all his ministers *become* wicked. (29:12)

No wonder so many in Trump's Cabinet resigned when they saw this happening. He replaced his Cabinet members who said things he didn't want to hear with others who agreed with him and praised him.

> When the wicked increase, transgression increases; but the righteous will see their fall. (29:16)

"Increase" can also be translated as "become great." This brings to mind Trump's continued undermining of our democratic institutions that help keep the balance of power in our republic, culminating with the attack on the Capitol and the 2020 election.

> Where there is no vision, the people are unrestrained, but happy is he who keeps the law. (29:18)

Make America Great Again (MAGA) was not a vision; it was only a con man's marketing line. And Trump certainly wasn't happy with his scores of failed attempts to bend election laws with legal suits to keep him in power and support his lies that he won the 2020 election by a landslide.

> Do you see a man who is hasty in his words?
> There is more hope for a fool than for him.
> (29:20)

Trump's rants and ramblings were often proof of his foolishness. The COVID virus was no worse than a flu and would go away when the summer came? His babbling during his speeches, interviews, and rallies is often very foolish. Trump's babbling in interviews about Putin's genius in invading Ukraine certainly is foolish for our nation's interest, but probably serves his and Putin's schemes quite well.

> An angry man stirs up strife, and a hot-tempered man abounds in transgression. (29:22)

The venting of anger is an important page in the conservative media playbook; remember, if you can hijack the amygdala, the brain's emotional center, the brain is not using the frontal lobes to think. Most conservative pundits and many conservative politicians use words to raise anger, disgust, or fear to keep the listener emotional rather than thoughtful. It certainly isn't the peace of Christ.

> A man's pride will bring him low, but a humble spirit will obtain honor. (29:23)

Trump is so prideful he raises himself by constantly honoring himself. Proverbs consistently reminds that God does not like pride.

> He who is a partner with a thief hates his own life; he hears the oath but tells nothing. (29:24)

The oath of office appears to mean little to those who enable Trump's wicked behaviors. I admire those in our government who, like Vice President Mike Pence, refused to follow Trump's orders when they conflicted with the oath they took to uphold our Constitution. Unlike Trump, they were faithful when they vowed, "So help me God."

> The fear of man brings a snare, but he who trusts in the LORD will be exalted. (29:25)

We must especially pray for our politicians who trust in the Lord rather than fearing Trump will support their opponents.

> Many seek the ruler's favor, but justice for man *comes* from the LORD. (29:26)

Too many who did Trump's bidding wound up being punished by the law.

An unjust man is abominable to the righteous, and he who is upright in the way is abominable to the wicked. (29:27)

The pardons that Trump gave to those who followed his bidding and then lied about it were an abomination of justice; they only needed a pardon because they were found guilty.

Proverbs 30

Proverbs 30:5 has been amazingly true in my life:

Every word of God is tested; He is a shield to those who take refuge in Him.

Sometimes that shield comes in the form of rebuke and/or conviction. Trump knows the value of using the word of God in to justify his actions—and so does the devil, as we see in Matthew, chapter 4, when he tries to tempt Jesus by quoting scripture.

Do not add to His words or He will reprove you, and you will be proved a liar. (30:6)

Please know that my comments on Proverbs are not meant to add to God's word; they are simply calling attention to verses that appear significant when His word is the lens used to look at the traits, behaviors, and words of Donald Trump.

There is a kind who is pure in his own eyes,
yet is not washed from his filthiness. (30:12)

Trump's quote of "great and unmatched wisdom" comes to mind here.

There is a kind—oh how lofty are his eyes!
And his eyelids are raised *in arrogance.* (30:13)

This is a common sight when Trump speaks at his rallies.

If you have been foolish in exalting yourself
or if you have plotted *evil, put your* hand on
your mouth. (30:32)

If Trump had any wisdom he would have done this long ago.

For the churning of milk produces butter,
and pressing the nose brings forth blood; so
the churning of anger produces strife. (30:33)

This verse is perhaps most applicable to Trump when he uses his rallies and social media to churn up the anger in his misled supporters, creating strife among the people of the United States of America, causing so many people from the right and the left to focus on what is wrong instead of what is right. Being grateful to God for how He has blessed our nation makes the joy of the Lord our strength!

Proverbs 31

Several verses in this chapter discuss the problems of alcohol. Trump's older brother struggled with it, and to his credit Trump learned to avoid it.

> Open your mouth for the mute, for the rights
> of all the unfortunate. (31:8)

Trump appeared to be more concerned with the rights of the fortunate; he knew their donations could pay for his campaigning.

> Open your mouth, judge righteously, and
> defend the rights of the afflicted and needy.
> (31:9)

Trump certainly isn't known for showing the wisdom of these last two verses. However, he is known for mocking people with disabilities.

AFTERWORD

So will My word be which goes forth from
My mouth; It will not return to Me empty,
without accomplishing what I desire, and
without succeeding in the matter for which
I sent it. (Isaiah 55:11)

Although this book has used the word of God primarily
from Proverbs as a lens through which to view Donald
Trump, there are many other books in the Old and New
Testaments that can be used this way. A well-known
passage from Corinthians is just one outstanding example
of such a lens for viewing Trump:

> Love is patient, love is kind. It is not jealous,
> is not pompous, it is not inflated, It is not
> rude, it does not seek its own interests, it is
> not quick-tempered, it does not brood over
> injury, it does not rejoice over wrongdoing
> but rejoices with the truth. (1 Corinthians
> 13:4–6)

Paul's description here of love is strikingly opposite to many of Trump's strongest traits.

May the wisdom in the book of Proverbs help you to understand the folly of following leaders or media that exhibit arrogance, deceitfulness, and mean-spirited scoffing to hijack your amygdala and make you angry, disgusted, or fearful.

Refuse to allow the political parties to manipulate you this way. Instead, use the frontal lobes of your brain to keep in mind this scripture from the book of James:

> Who among you is wise and understanding? Let him show by his good behavior his deeds in the gentleness of wisdom. But if you have bitter jealousy and selfish ambition in your heart, do not be arrogant and so lie against the truth. This wisdom is not that which comes down from above, but is earthly, natural, demonic. For where jealousy and selfish ambition exist, there is disorder and every evil thing. But the wisdom from above is first pure, then peaceable, gentle, reasonable, full of mercy and good fruits, unwavering, without hypocrisy. And the seed whose fruit is righteousness is sown in peace by those who make peace. (James 3:13–18)

⁵ But if any of you lacks wisdom, let him ask of God, who gives to all generously and without reproach, and it will be given to him. ⁶ But he must ask in faith without any doubting, for the one who doubts is like the surf of the sea, driven and tossed by the wind. ⁷ For that man ought not to expect that he will receive anything from the Lord, ⁸ *being* a double-minded man, unstable in all his ways. (James 1:5-8)

¹⁹ *This* you know, my beloved brethren. But everyone must be quick to hear, slow to speak *and* slow to anger; ²⁰ for the anger of man does not achieve the righteousness of God. ²¹ Therefore, putting aside all filthiness and *all* that remains of wickedness, in humility receive the word implanted, which is able to save your souls. ²² But prove yourselves doers of the word, and not merely hearers who delude themselves. ²³ For if anyone is a hearer of the word and not a doer, he is like a man who looks at his natural face in a mirror; ²⁴ for *once* he has looked at himself and gone away, he has immediately forgotten what kind of person he was. ²⁵ But one who looks intently at the perfect law, the *law* of liberty, and abides by it, not having become

a forgetful hearer but an effectual doer, this man will be blessed in what he does. [26] If anyone thinks himself to be religious, and yet does not bridle his tongue but deceives his own heart, this man's religion is worthless. (James 1:19-26)

Paul describes another way this peace comes to our brains in his letter to the Philippians:

Rejoice in the Lord always; again I will say, rejoice! Let your gentle *spirit* be known to all men. The Lord is near. Be anxious for nothing, but in everything by prayer and supplication with thanksgiving let your requests be made known to God. And the peace of God, which surpasses all comprehension, will guard your hearts and your minds in Christ Jesus.

Finally, brethren, whatever is true, whatever is honorable, whatever is right, whatever is pure, whatever is lovely, whatever is of good repute, if there is any excellence and if anything worthy of praise, dwell on these things. The things you have learned and received and heard and seen in me, practice these things, and the God of peace will be with you. (Philippians 4:4–9)

The Bible really is a book of God's love for us. Here too is another important verse from the Bible that clearly shows Trump is not what God wants his people to follow, as Jesus commands us to love one another:

> "A new commandment I give to you, that you *love one another*, even as I have *loved* you, that you also *love one another*. By this all men will know that you are My disciples, if you have *love for one another*." (John 13:34–35, emphasis mine)

Then in the next chapter of John, Jesus is quoted again:

> "If you love Me, you will keep My commandments." (John 14:15)

God willing, another book bringing other quotes from the Bible that shine the light of truth on the abominable behaviors of Donald Trump is coming. Until then, pray for the unity of our nation, seek through scripture to better know our Lord and how much he loves us, and love one another as Jesus has commanded. This is the key for the United States of America to come together so that the amazing blessings of God continue and His wrath is stopped.

ABOUT THE AUTHOR

While Israel remained at Shittim, the people began to play the harlot with the daughters of Moab. ² For they invited the people to the sacrifices of their gods, and the people ate and bowed down to their gods. ³ So Israel joined themselves to Baal of Peor, and the LORD was angry against Israel. ⁴ The LORD said to Moses, "Take all the leaders of the people and execute them in broad daylight before the LORD, so that the fierce anger of the LORD may turn away from Israel." ⁵ So Moses said to the judges of Israel, "Each of you slay his men who have joined themselves to Baal of Peor." ⁶ Then behold, one of the sons of Israel came and brought to his relatives a Midianite woman, in the sight of Moses and in the sight of all the congregation of the sons of Israel, while they were weeping at the doorway of the tent of meeting. ⁷ When **Phinehas** the son of Eleazar, the son of Aaron the priest, saw it, he arose from the midst of the congregation and took a spear in his hand, ⁸ and he went after the man of Israel into the tent and pierced both of them through, the man of Israel and the woman, through the body. So the plague on the sons of Israel was checked.

⁹ Those who died by the plague were 24,000. ¹⁰ Then the LORD spoke to Moses, saying, ¹¹ **"Phinehas** the son of Eleazar, the son of Aaron the priest, has turned away My wrath from the sons of Israel in that he was jealous with My jealousy among them, so that I did not destroy the sons of Israel in My jealousy. ¹² Therefore say, 'Behold, I give him My covenant of peace; ¹³ and it shall be for him and his descendants after him, a covenant of a perpetual priesthood, because he was jealous for his God and made atonement for the sons of Israel.'" Numbers 25:1-13 (NASB 1995)

Printed in the United States
by Baker & Taylor Publisher Services